Practice drawing basic lines. Trace each line from ●→ to ●.

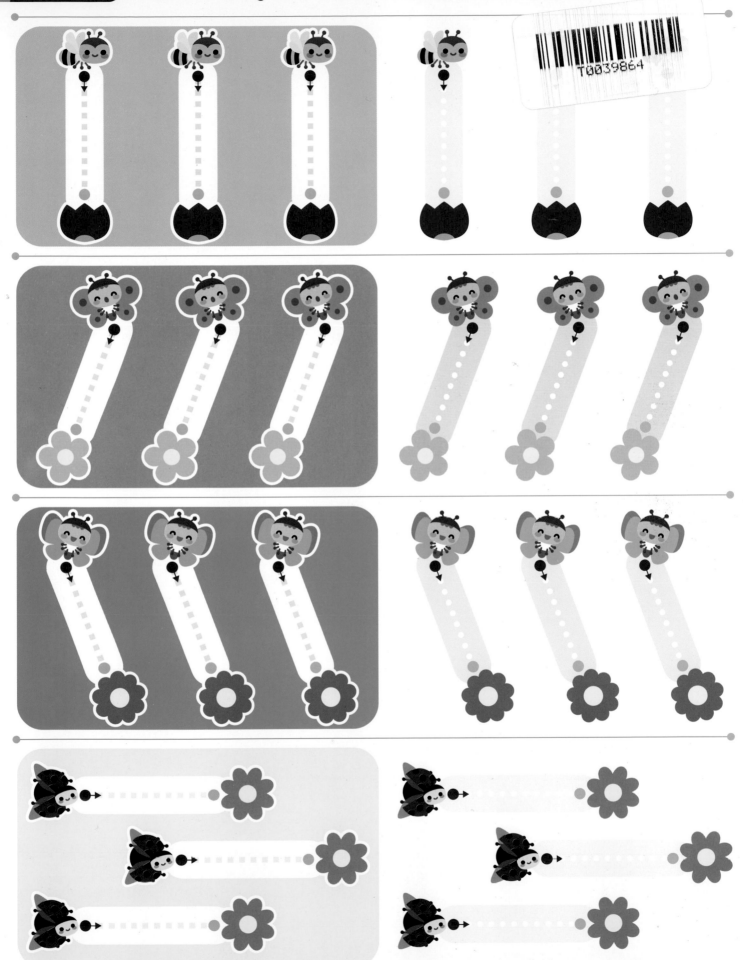

2

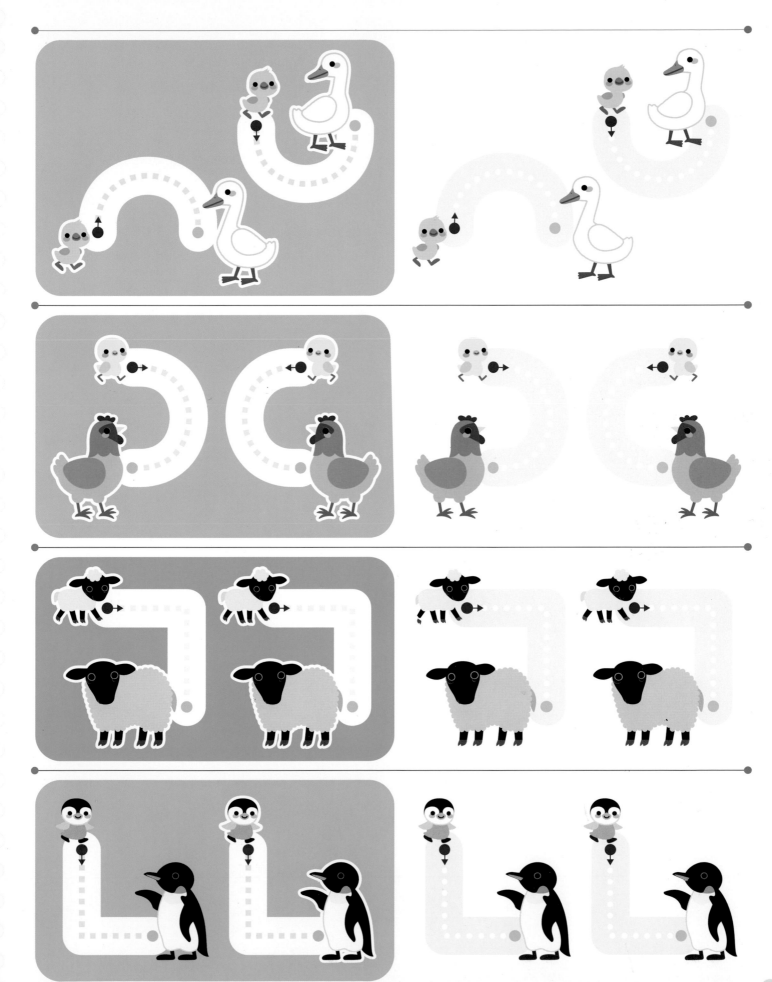

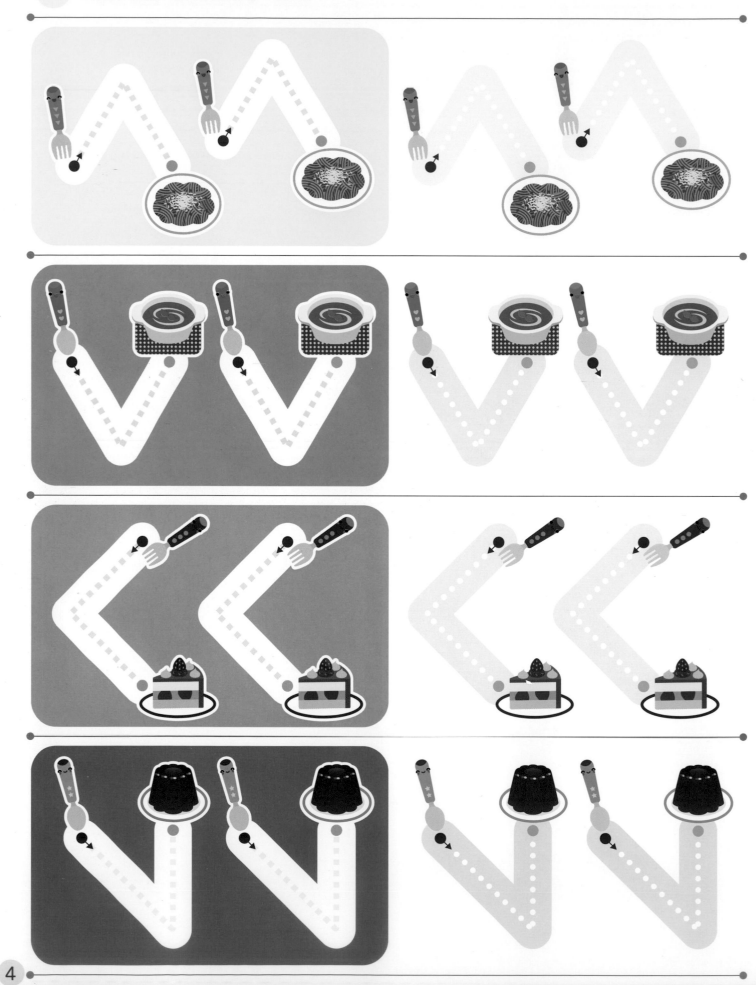

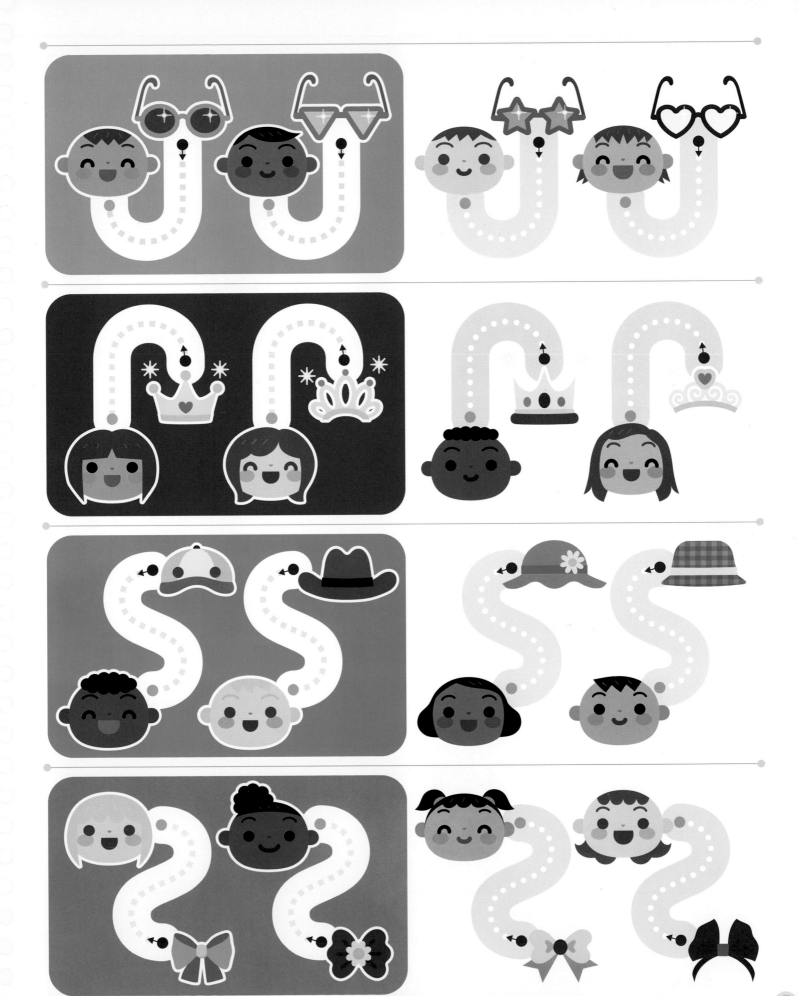

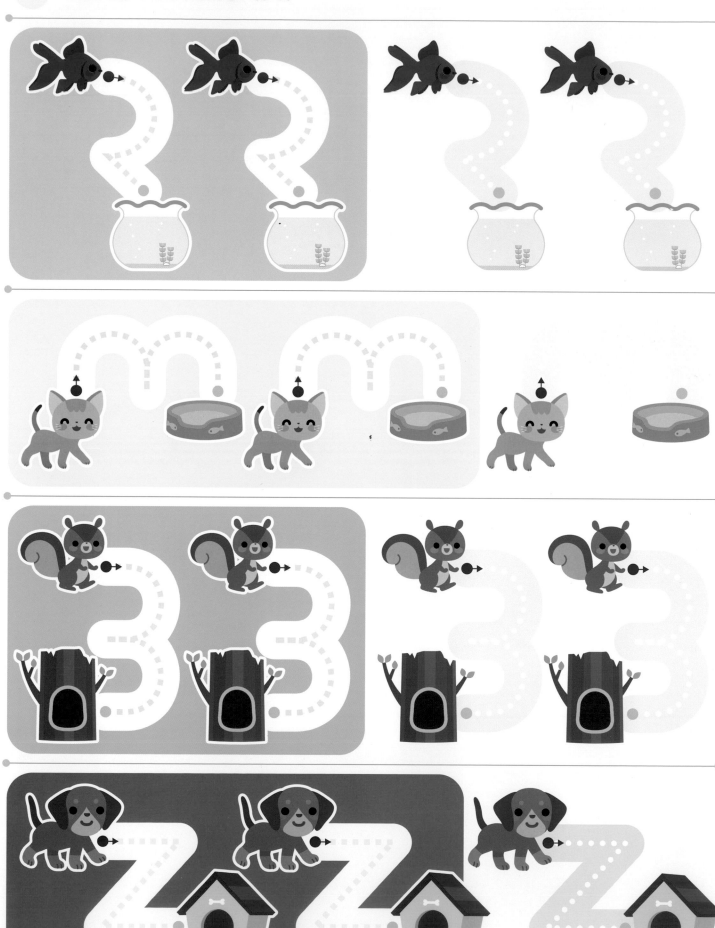

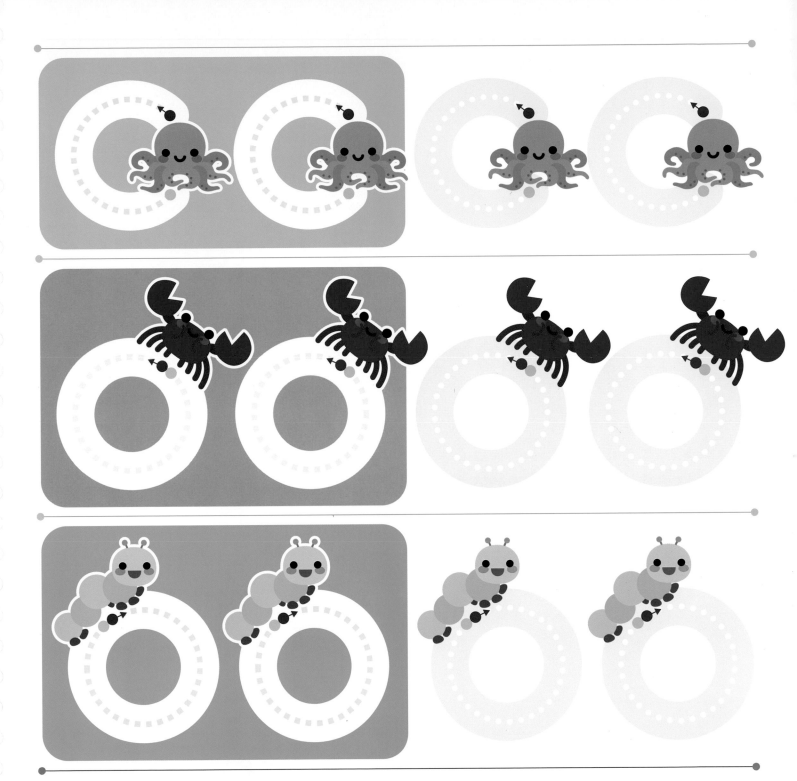

Draw a dot on each duck's eye.

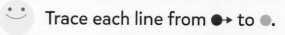
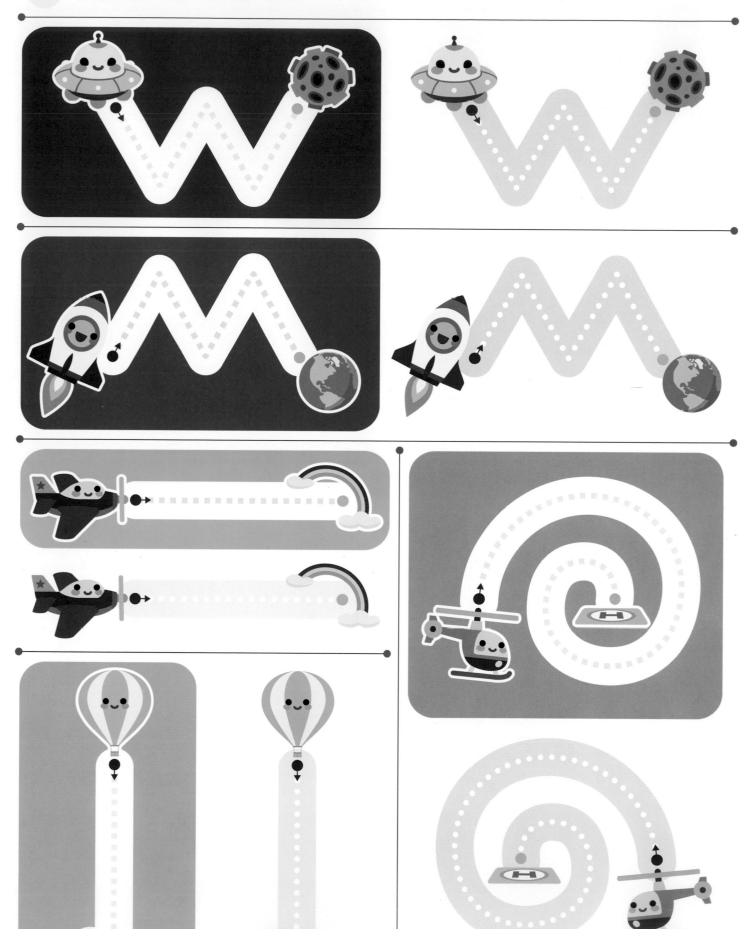

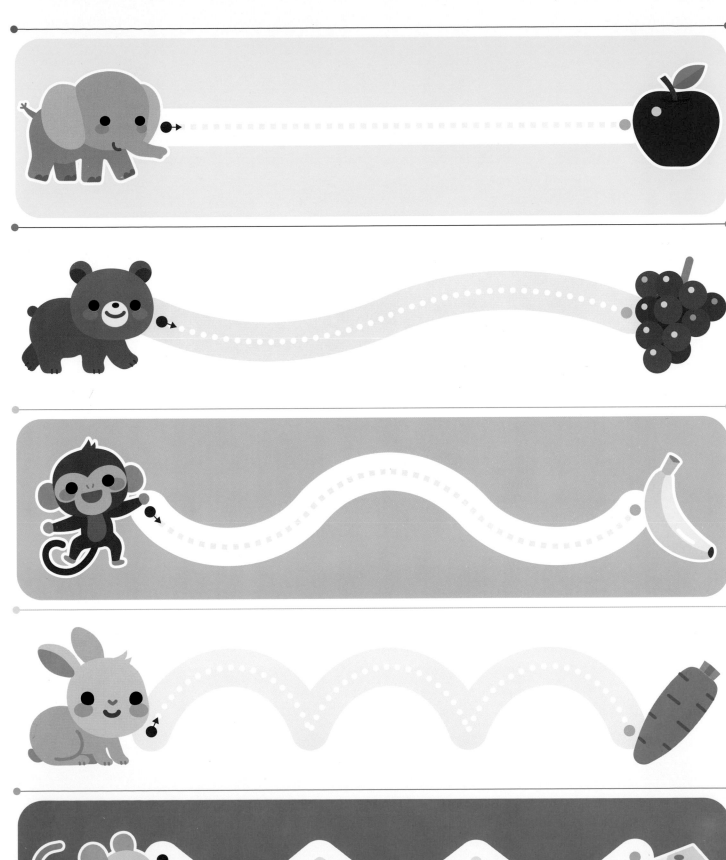

Trace each letter.

Aa

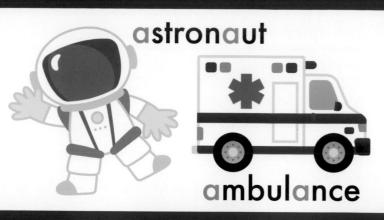

astronaut

ambulance

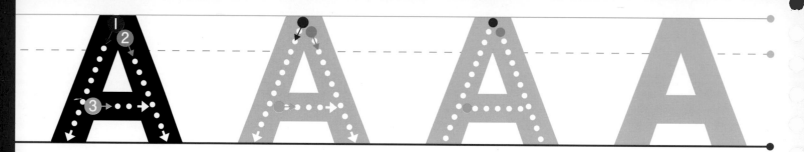

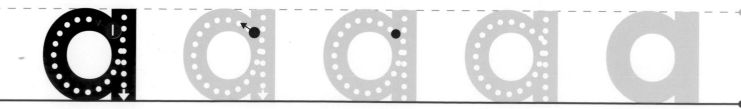

airplane

alligator

ant

apple

A A A A

A A A

apple

alligator

B b

bird   banana

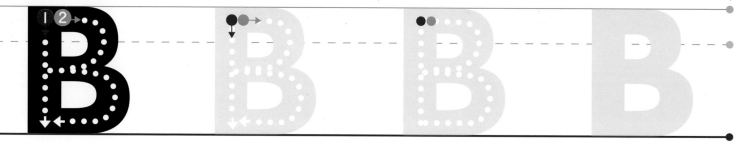

bus

bee

bear

ball

B b B b

B b

b ee

b us

car

carrot

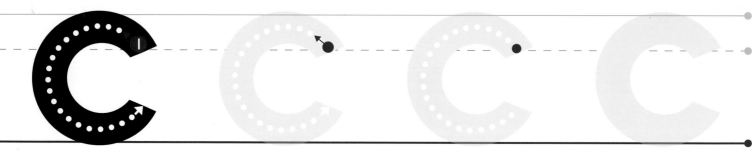

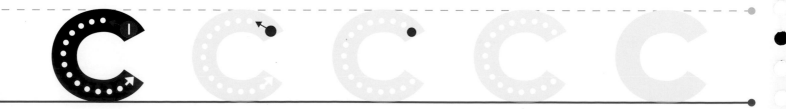

14

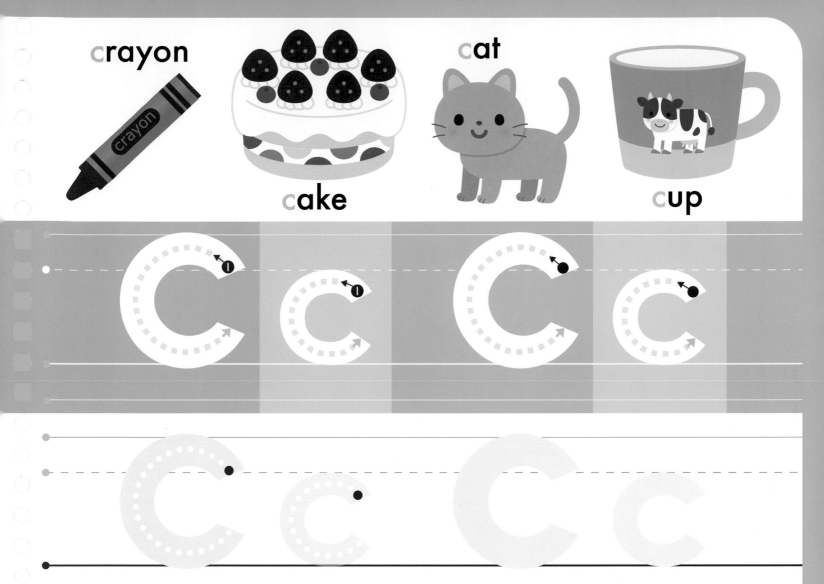

crayon

cake

cat

cup

C c C c C c C c

C c C c C c C c

cat

cup

D d

dog

doll

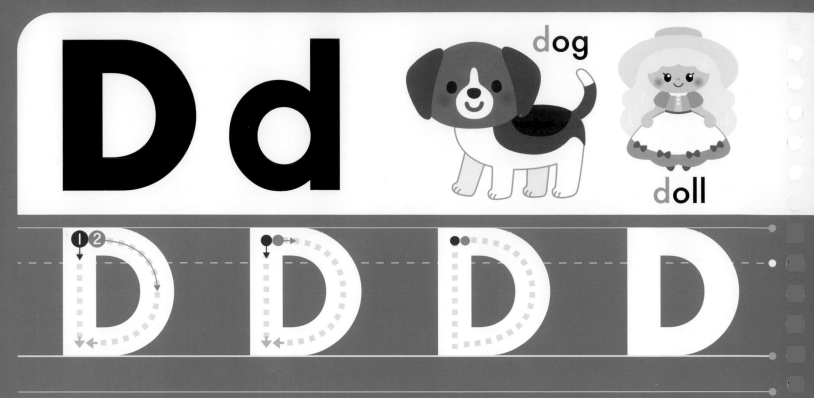

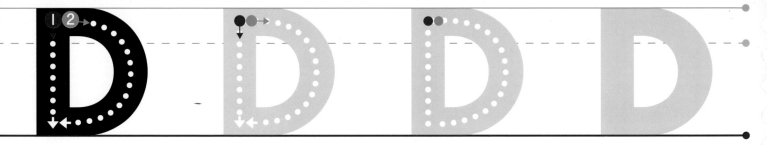

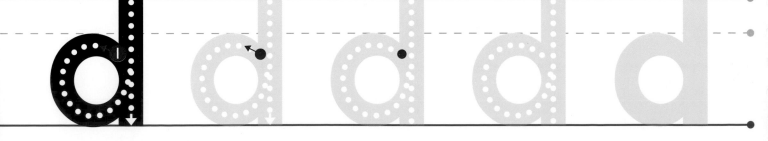

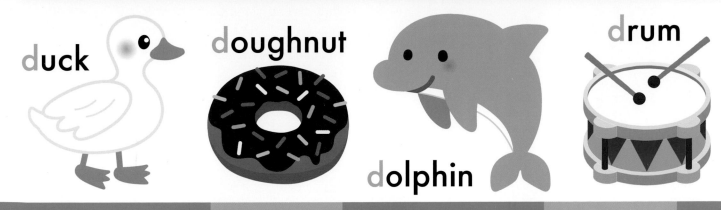

duck

doughnut

dolphin

drum

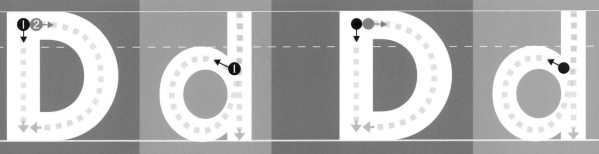

D d D d

D d D d

dog

duck

E e

eggplant

Earth

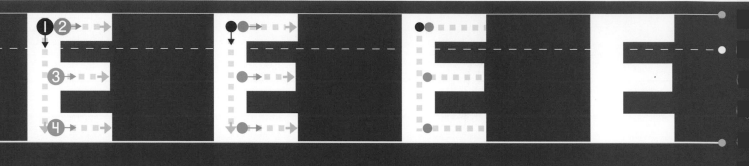

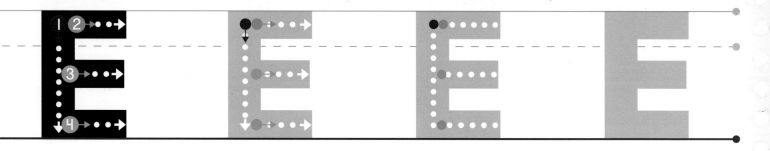

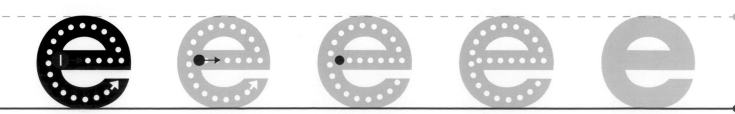

eye

ear

elephant

egg

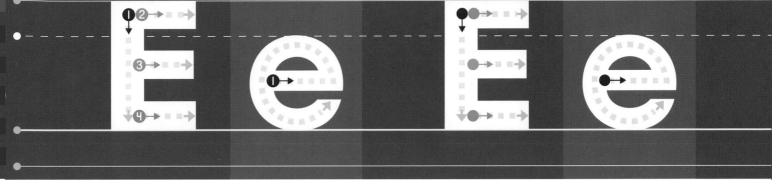

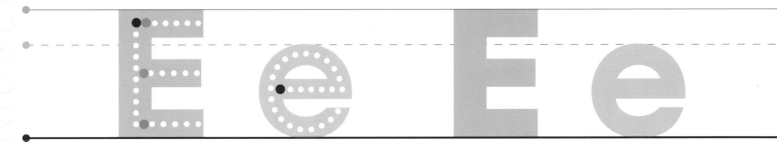

egg

Earth

F f

flower

fish

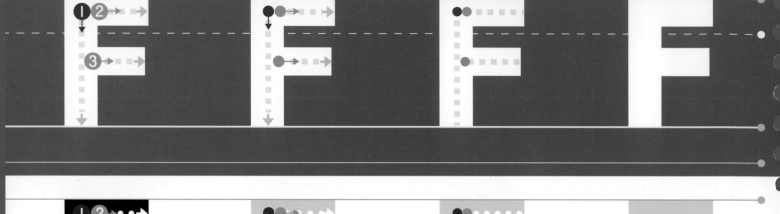

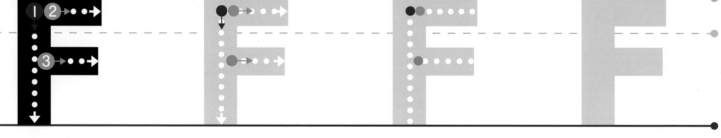

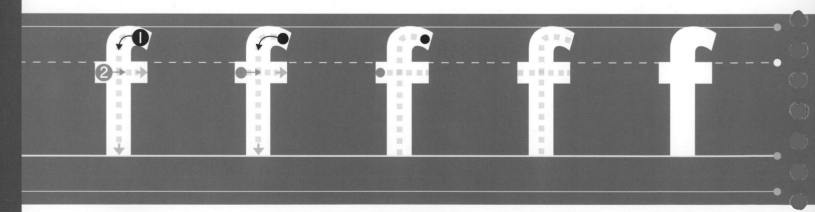

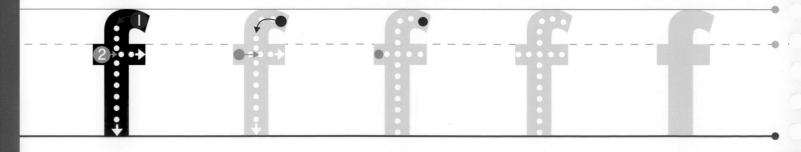

feet

fork

frog

fire engine

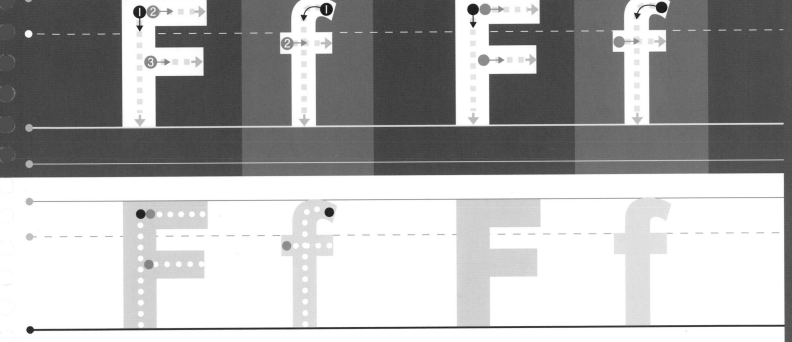

fish

frog

G g

ghost

guitar

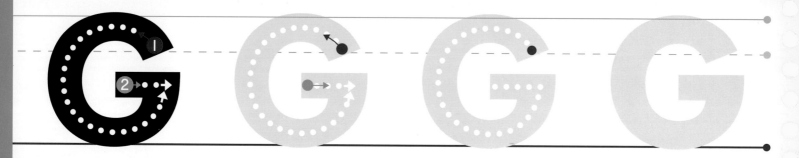

gift

glasses

giraffe

grapes

G g G g

G g G g

gift

grapes

Hh

hat

hedgehog

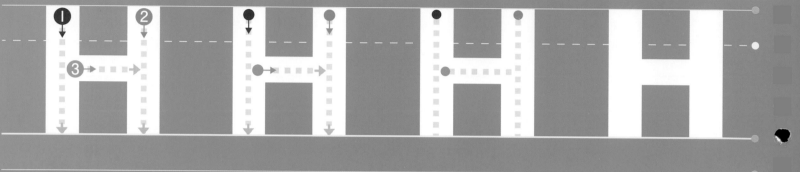

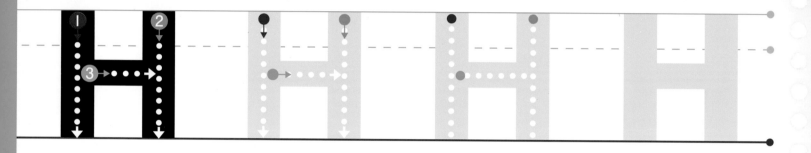

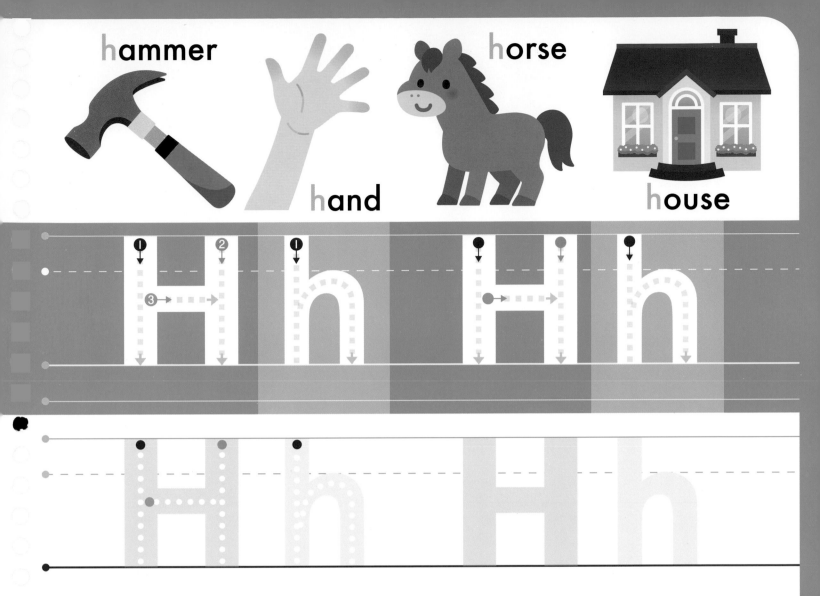

hammer

hand

horse

house

H h H h

H h H h

hat

horse

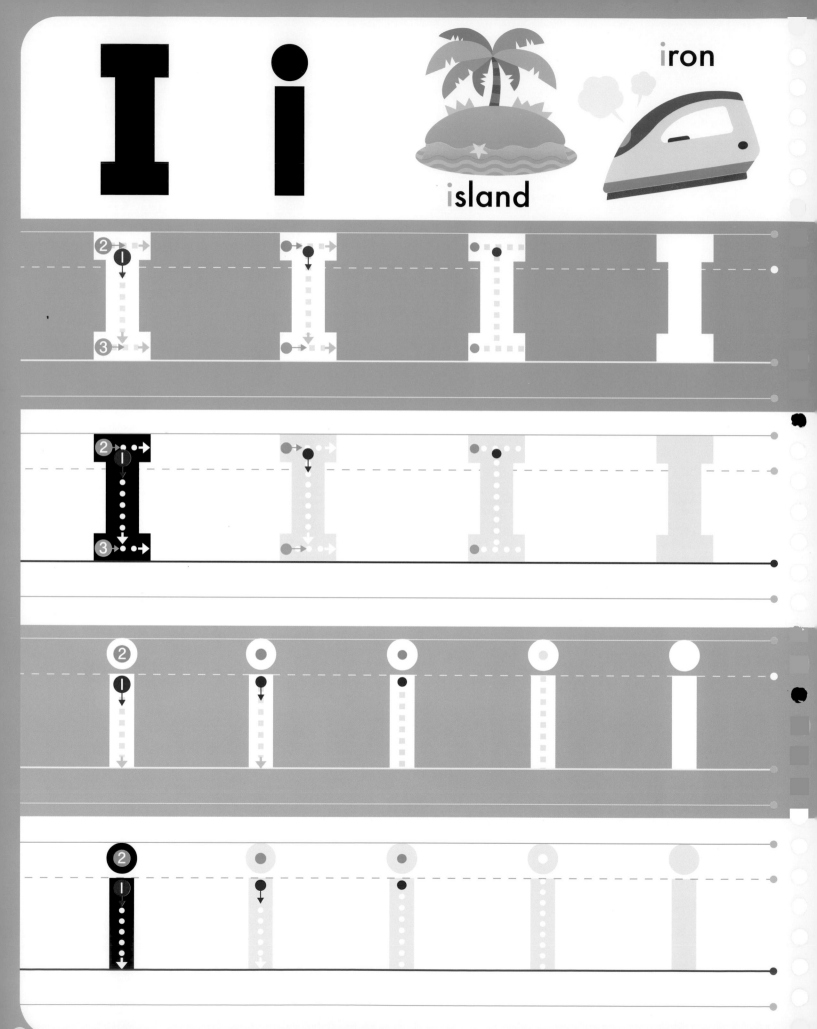

I i

island

iron

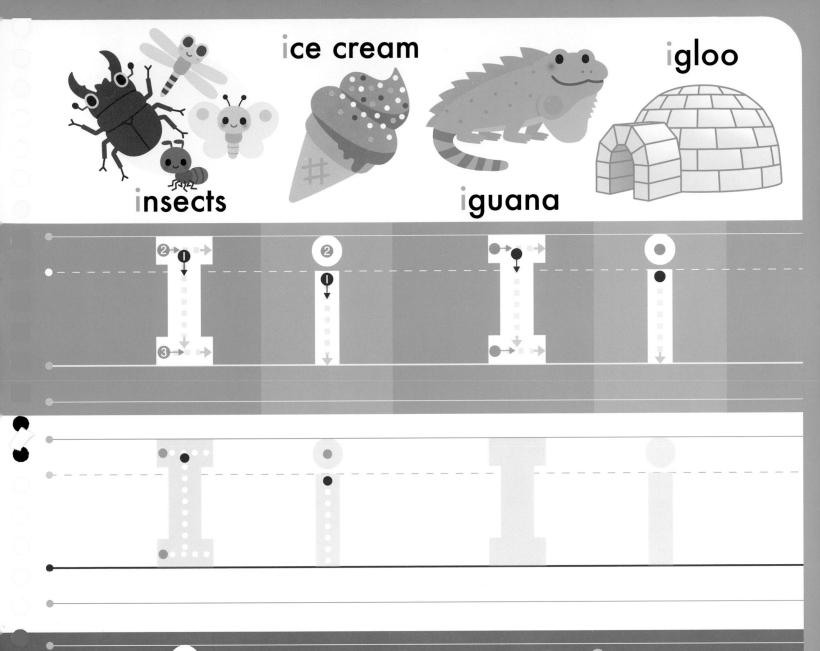

insects

ice cream

iguana

igloo

iron

insects

J j

jellyfish

jam

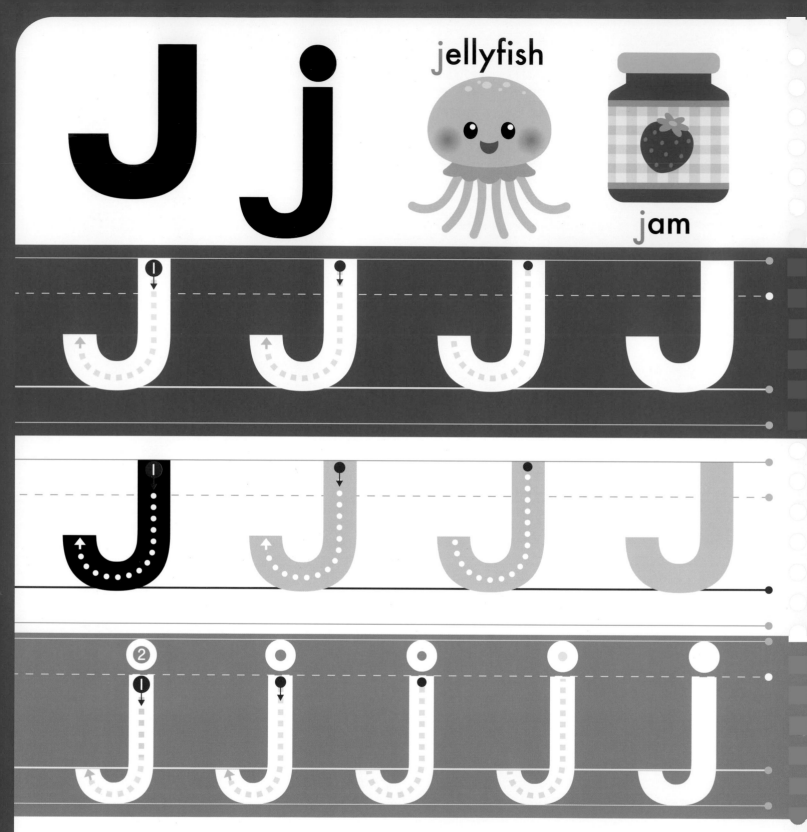

jeans

jaguar

jet

juice

juice

jam

29

K k

kangaroo

kiwi

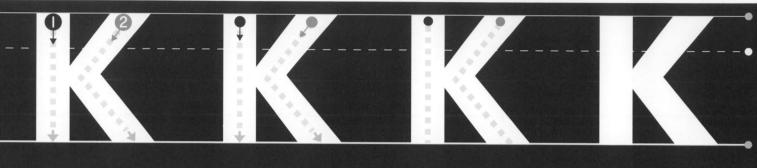

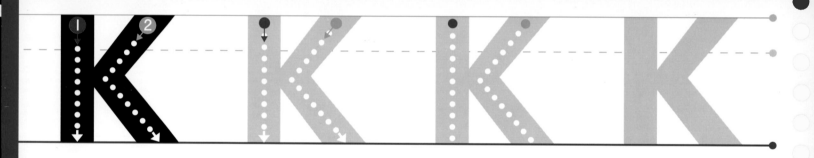

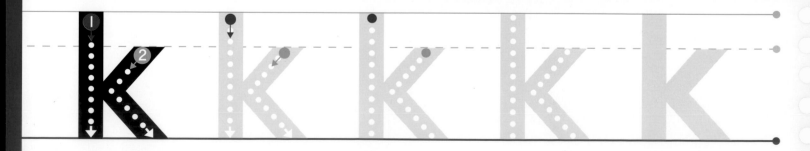

king

kite

koala

key

K k K k K k

K k K k

koala

kite

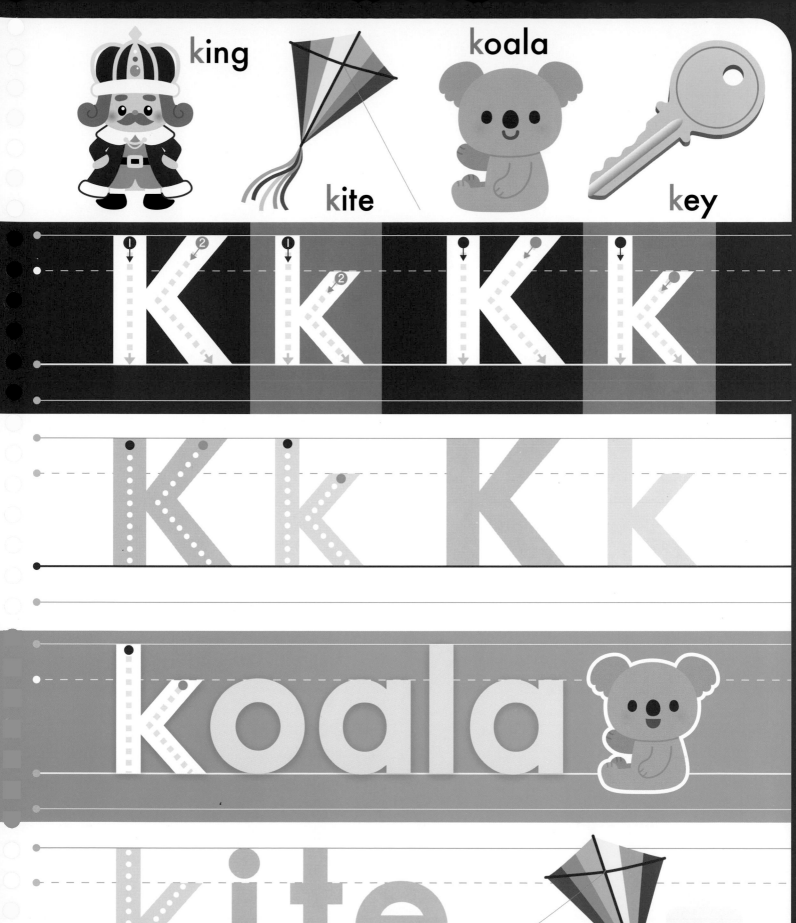

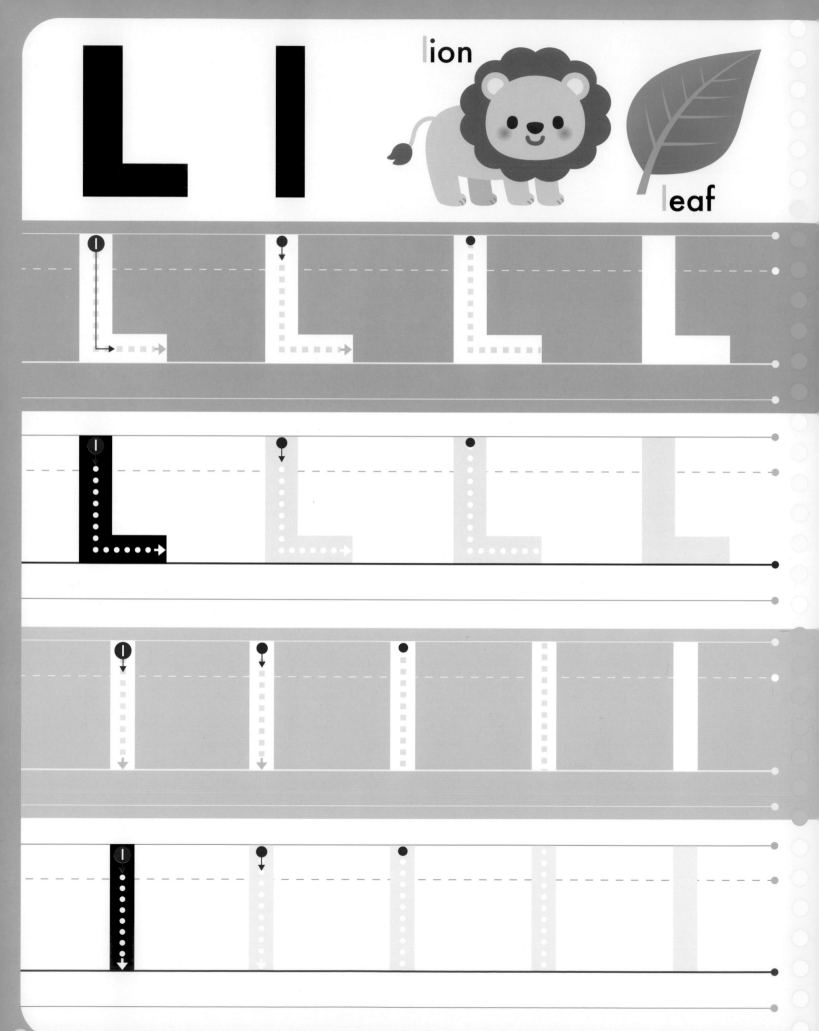

L l

lion

leaf

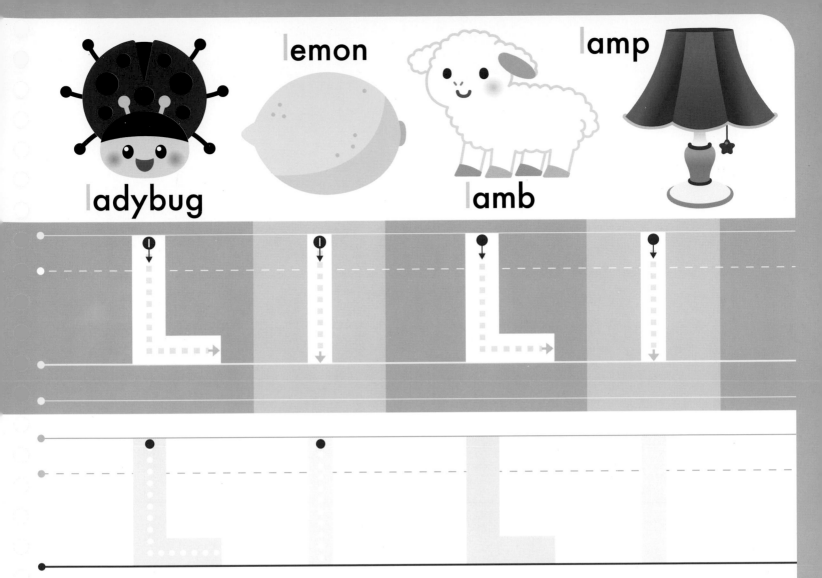

ladybug

lemon

lamb

lamp

lion

lamp

33

M m

monkey

milk

M M M M M

M M M M

m m m m m

m m m m

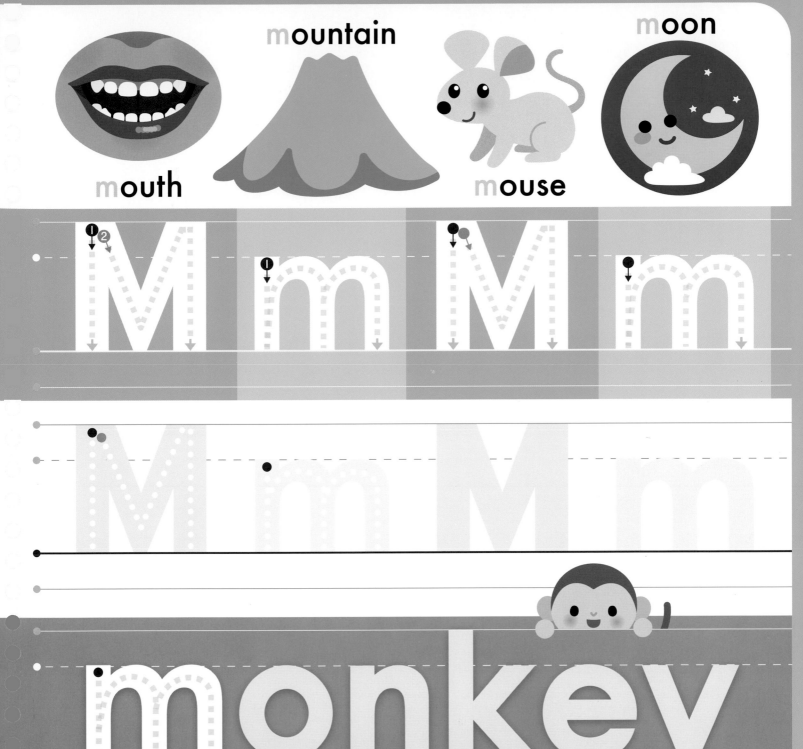

mouth

mountain

mouse

moon

M m M m

M m M m

monkey

mouse

N n

necklace

nest

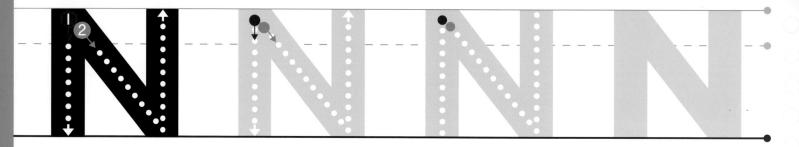

nail

night

nose

net

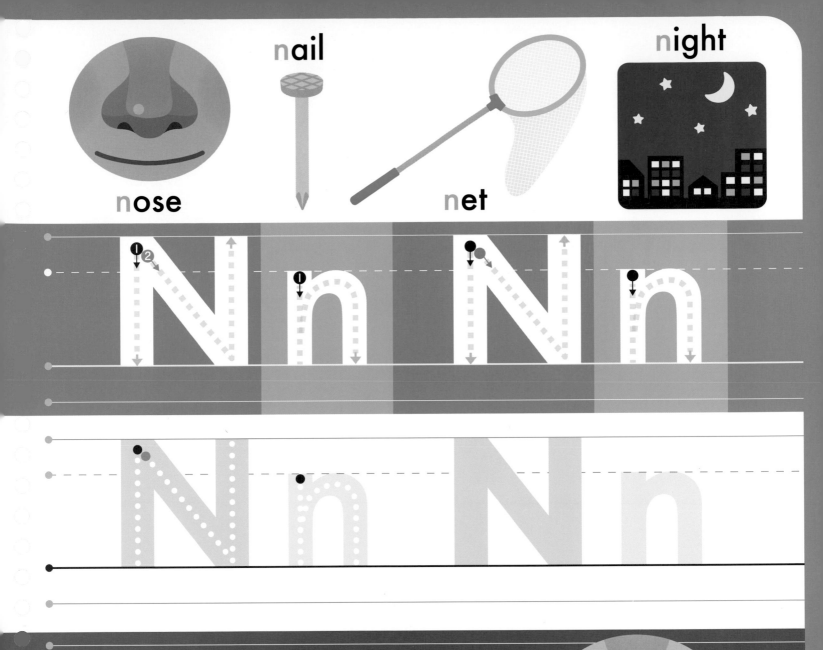

Nn Nn

Nn Nn

nose

net

otter onion

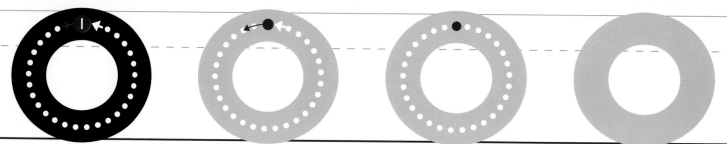

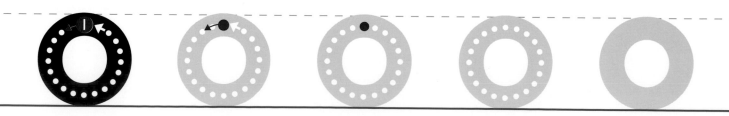

owl

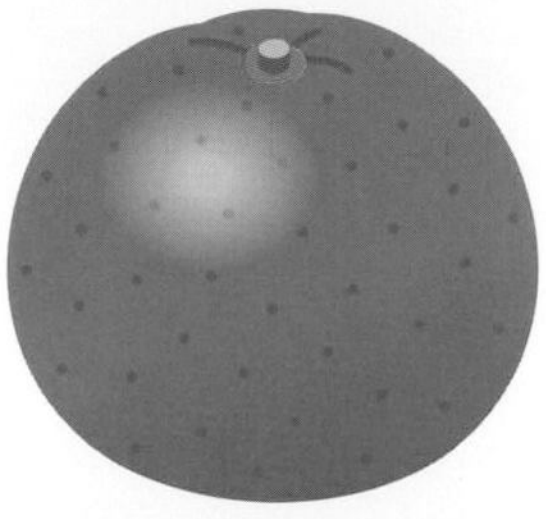

orange

octopus

ocean

O o O o

O o O o

orange

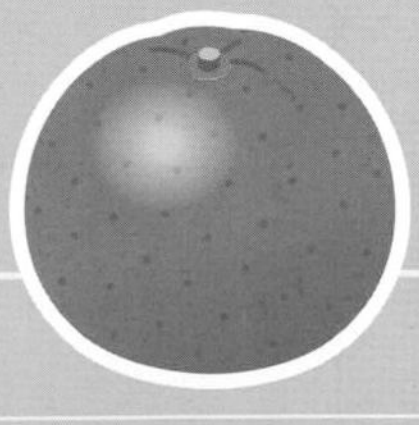

octopus

P p

panda

pear

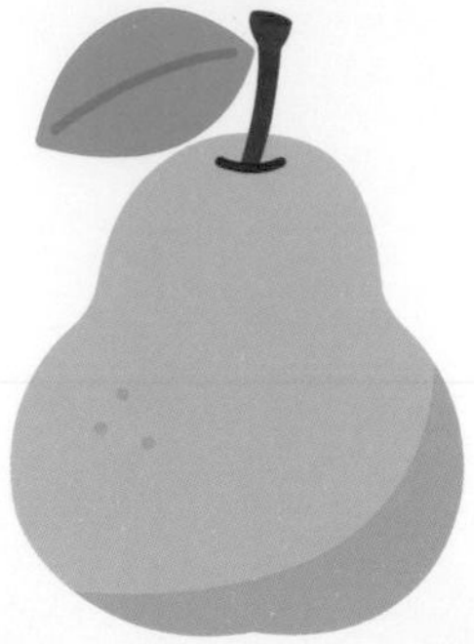

P P P P P

P P P P

p p p p p

p p p p

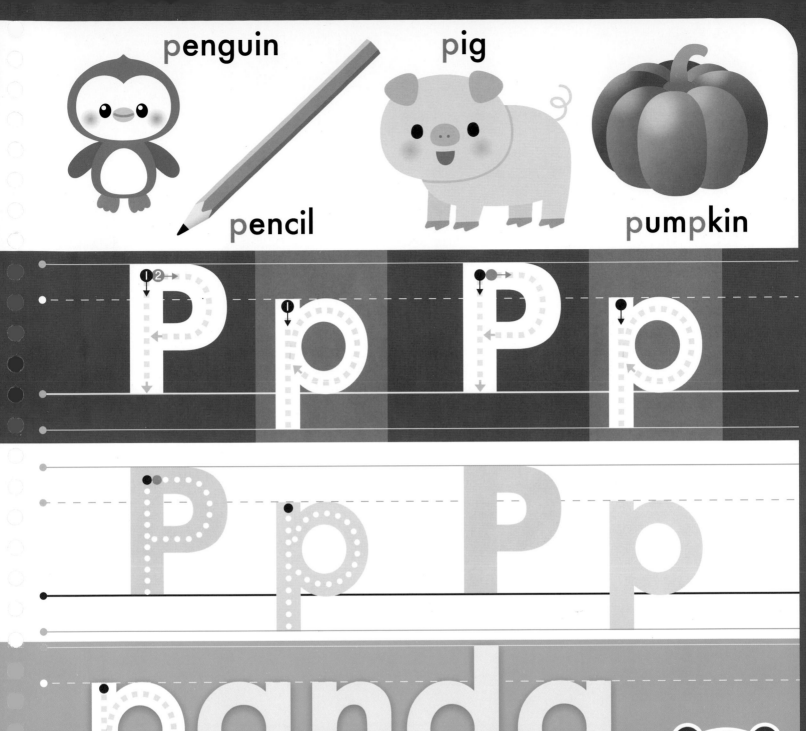

penguin

pencil

pig

pumpkin

P p P p P p P p

P p P p P p

panda

pig

Qq

quail

quilt

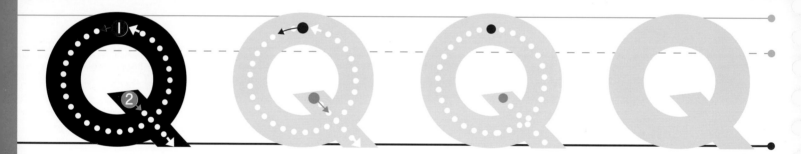

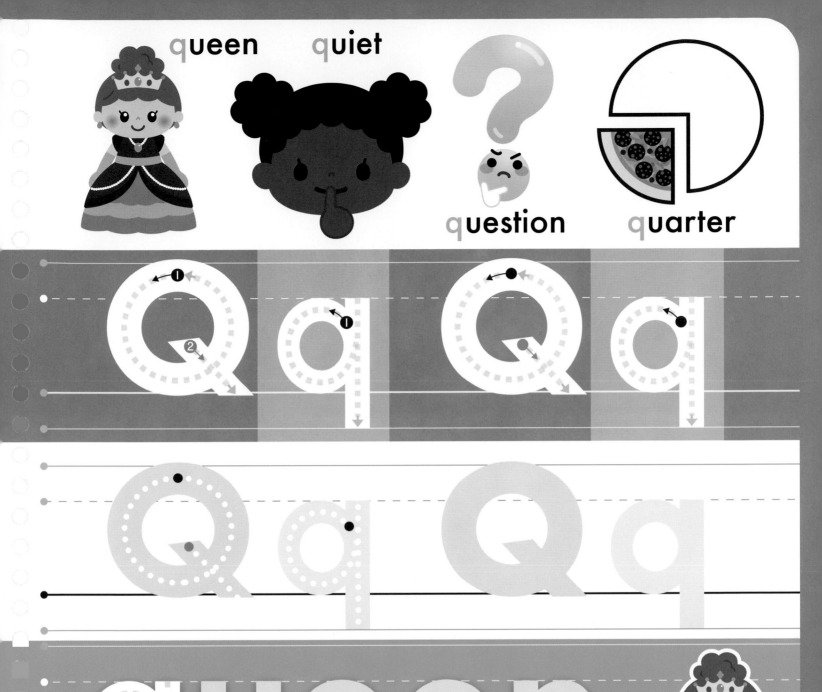

queen   quiet

question   quarter

queen

quiet

R r

robot

rose

44

rocket

ring

rabbit

rainbow

R r R r

R r R r

rabbit

rose

S s

strawberry

snake

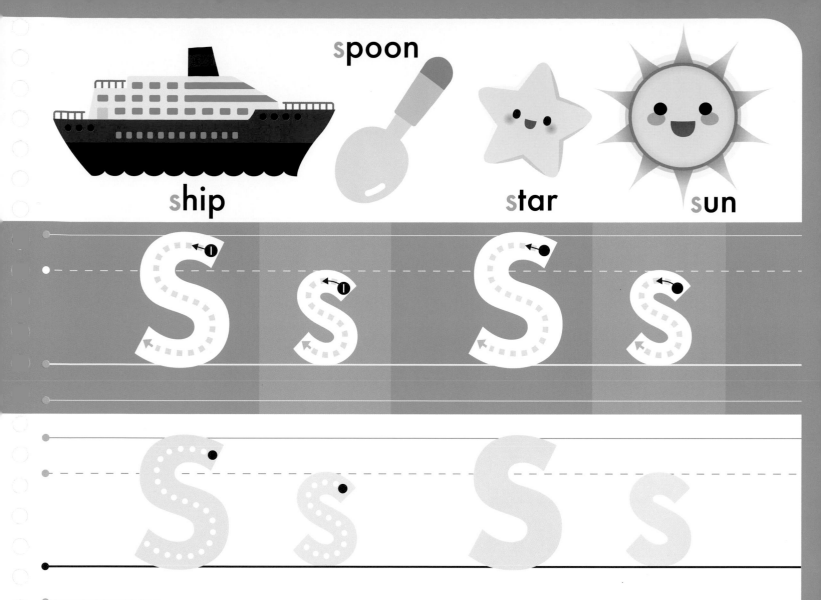

spoon

ship

star

sun

s S s S

S s S s

star

snake

T t

tiger

tooth

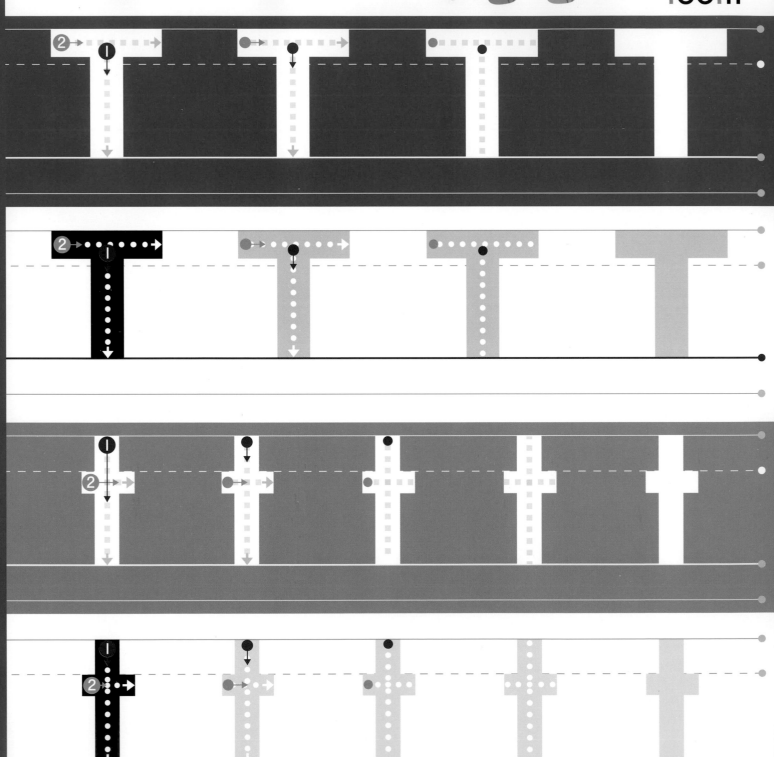

tomato

tree

turtle

train

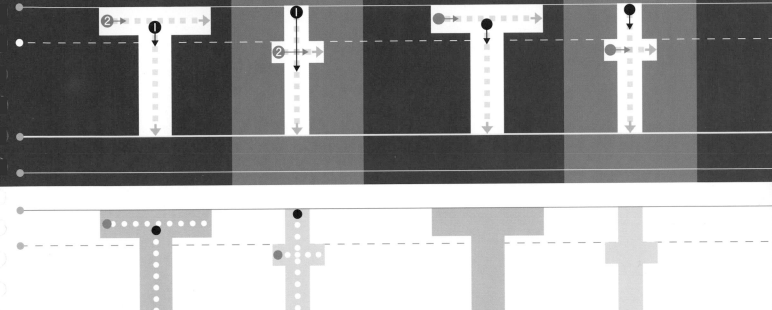

tiger

tree

U u

unicorn

umbrella

U U U U

U U U U

U U U U U

U U U U

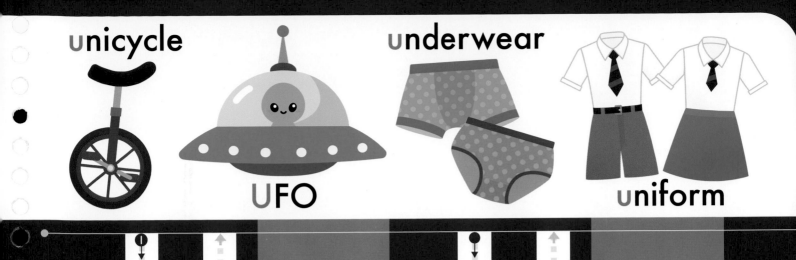

unicycle

UFO

underwear

uniform

U u U u U u U u

U u U u

unicorn

umbrella

V v

vegetables

vase

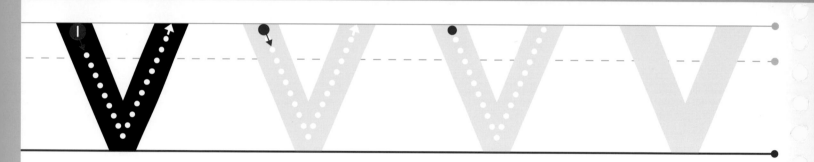

52

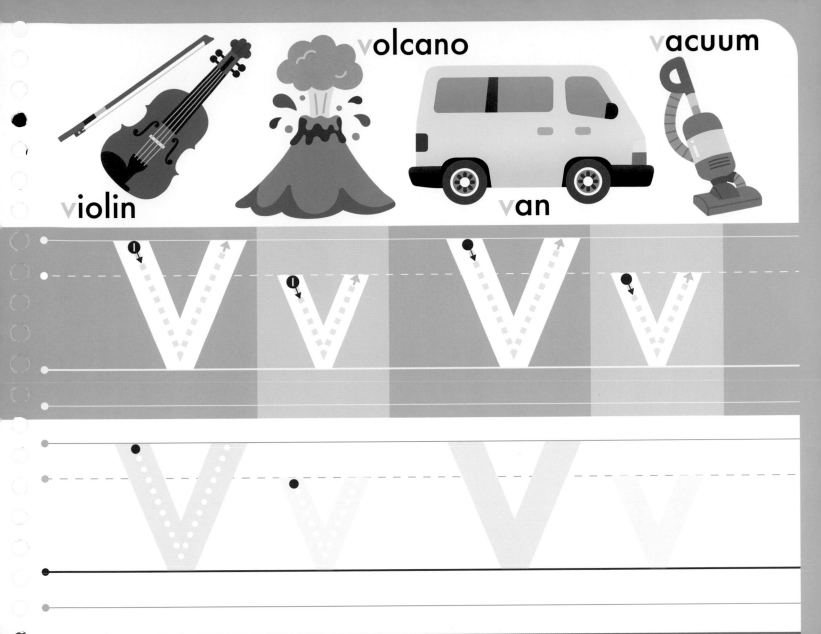

violin

volcano

van

vacuum

V v v v v

v v

van

violin

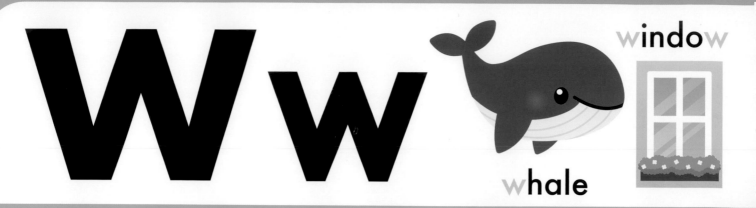

window

whale

watermelon

watch

wolf

wagon

W w W w W w

W w W w W w

whale

wolf

X x

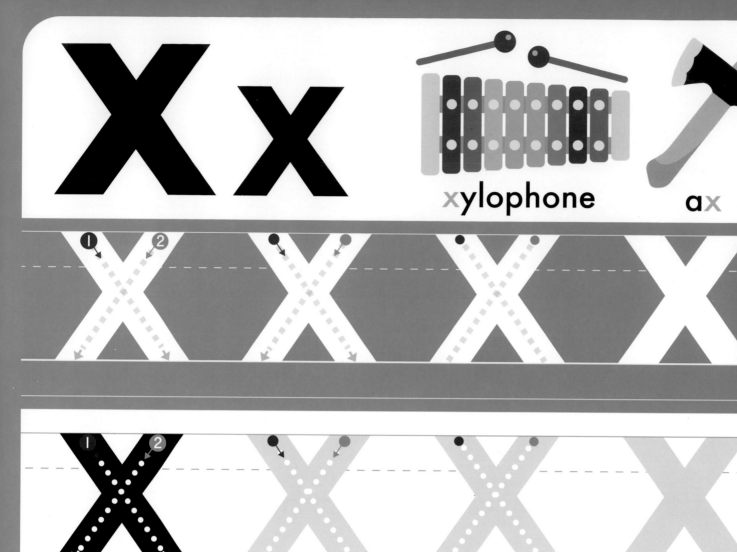

xylophone

ax

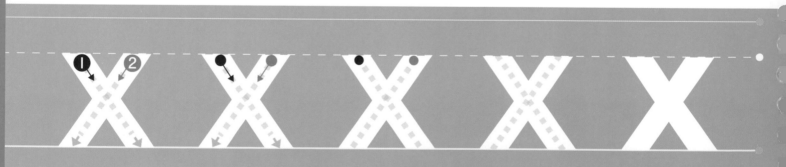

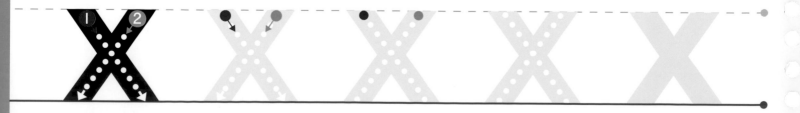

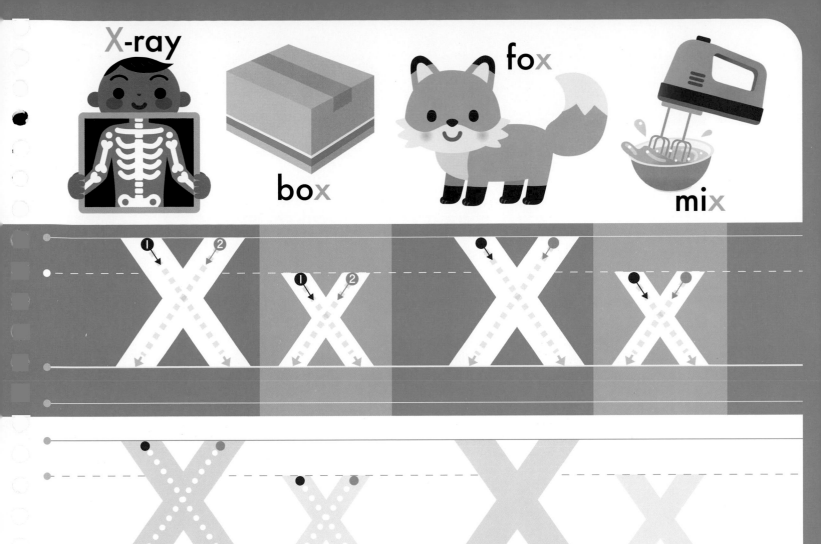

X-ray

box

fox

mix

X x

X-ray

box

Y y

yogurt

yarn

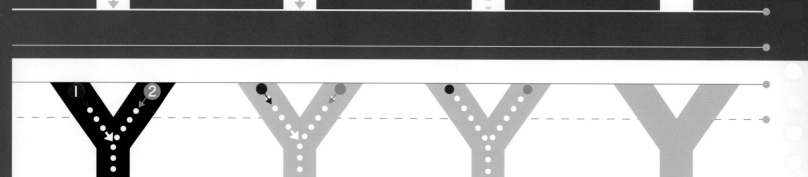

yo-yo

yacht

yam

yak

Y y Y y

Y y Y y

yarn

yogurt

Z z

zebra

zero

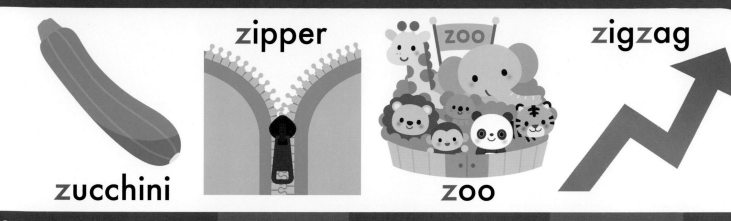

zucchini

zipper

zoo

zigzag

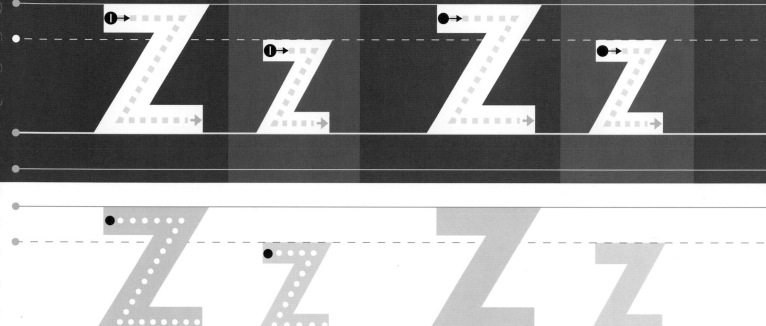

zebra

zipper

Trace the letters from A to Z. Say the word below each letter.

A a   B b   C c

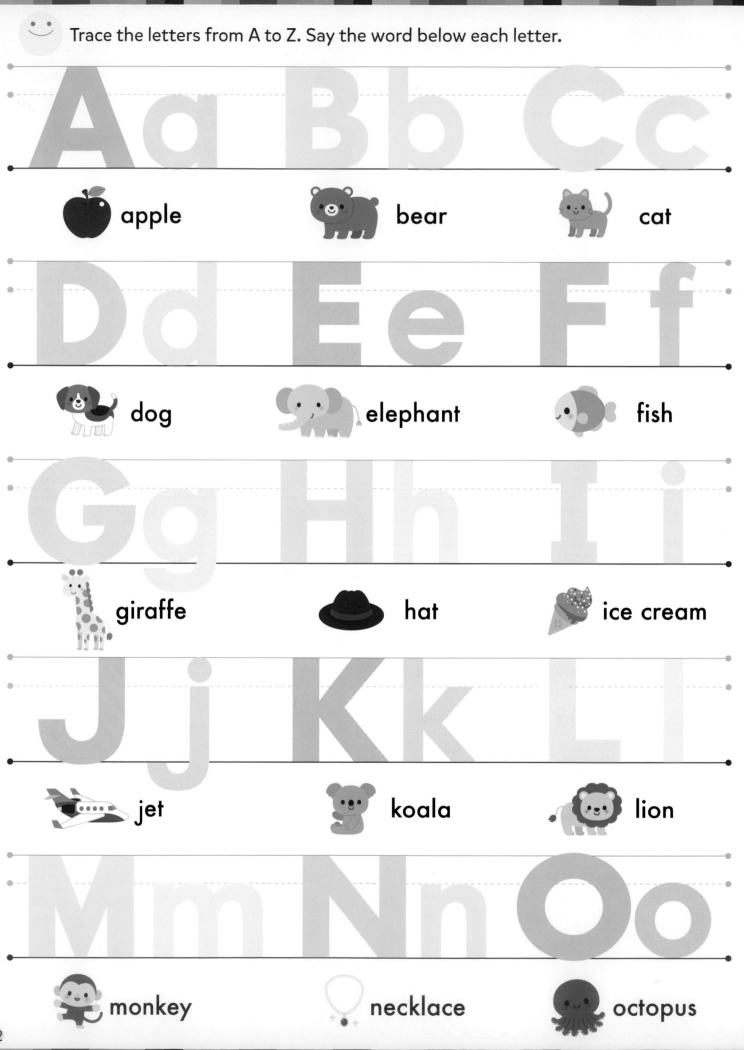

apple   bear   cat

D d   E e   F f

dog   elephant   fish

G g   H h   I i

giraffe   hat   ice cream

J j   K k   L l

jet   koala   lion

M m   N n   O o

monkey   necklace   octopus

Pp Qq Rr

penguin   queen   rabbit

Ss Tt Uu

strawberry   tree   umbrella

Vv Ww Xx

violin   whale   X-ray

Yy Zz

yo-yo   zebra

Trace each number. Then, trace each letter that spells the number.

one

Color the circle and count it.

⭐ Trace I whale.

⭐ Circle the group of I.

example

64

2

two

Color the circles and count them.

2 2 2 2

Trace 2 trains.

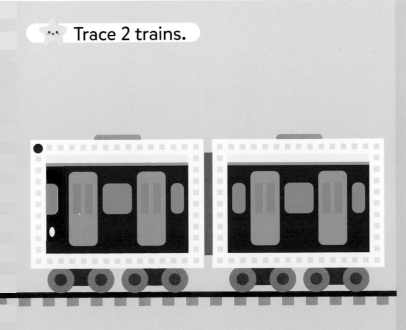

Circle the group of 2.

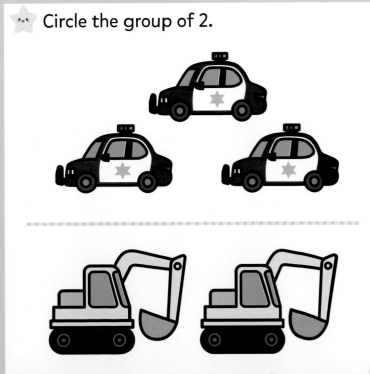

3

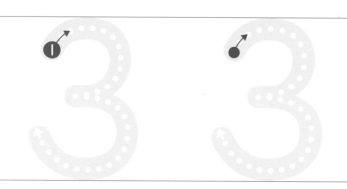

⭐ Trace 3 eggs.

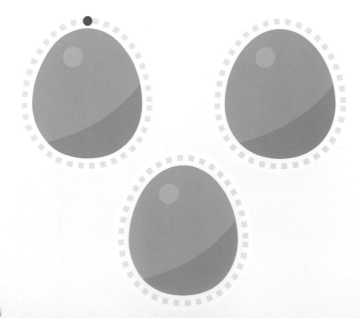

⭐ Circle the group of 3.

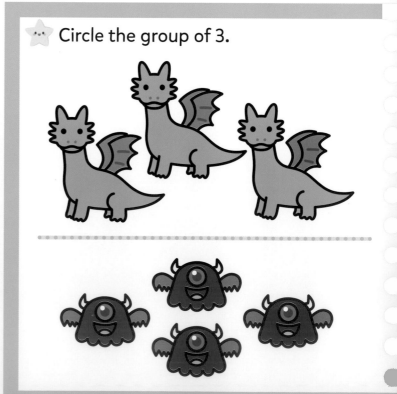

4

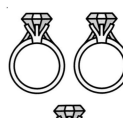

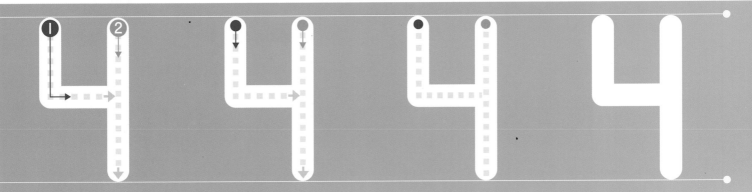

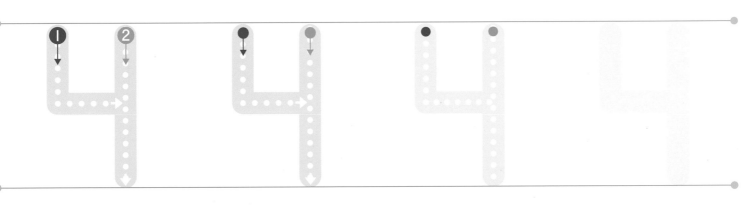

⭐ Trace 4 hats.

⭐ Circle the group of 4.

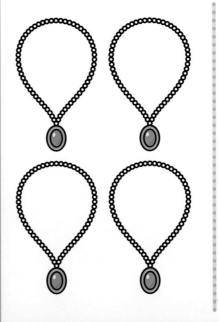

5

 five

Color the circles and count them.

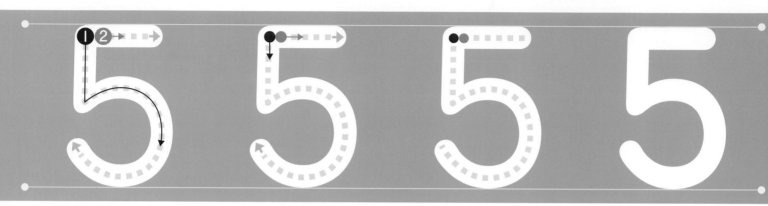

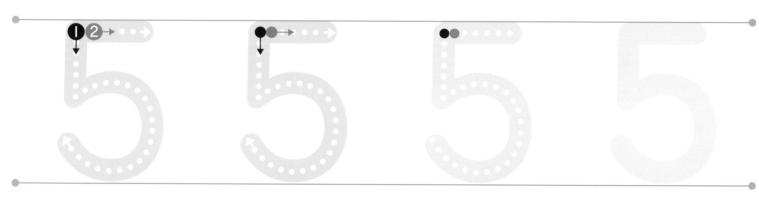

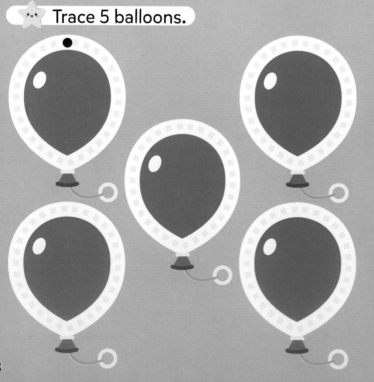

Trace 5 balloons.

Circle the group of 5.

6

six

Color the circles and count them.

⭐ Trace 6 trees.

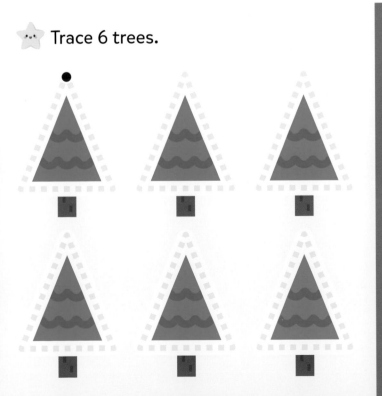

⭐ Circle the group of 6.

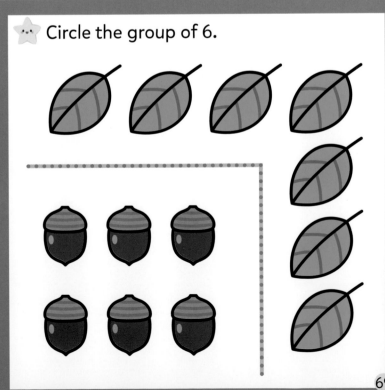

7

 seven

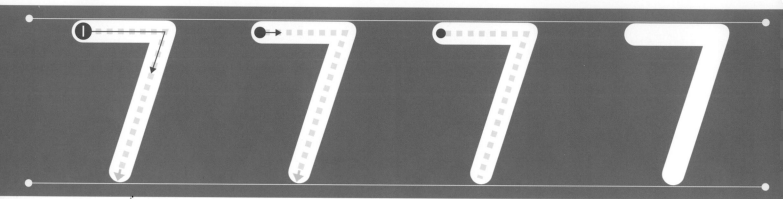

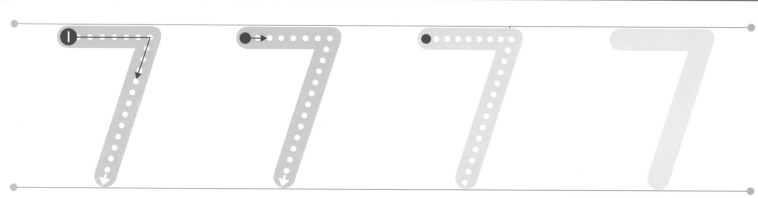

⭐ Trace 7 jellyfish.

⭐ Circle the group of 7.

8 eight

Color the circles and count them.

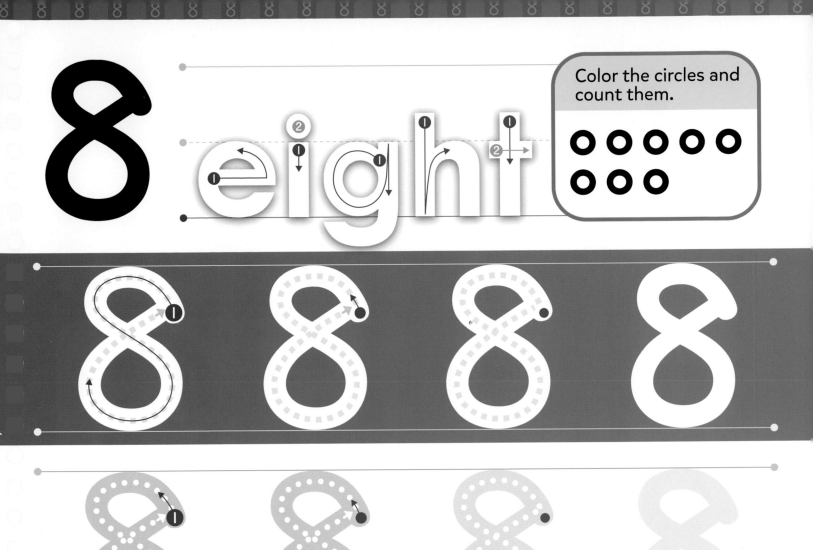

Trace 8 zucchini.

Circle the group of 8.

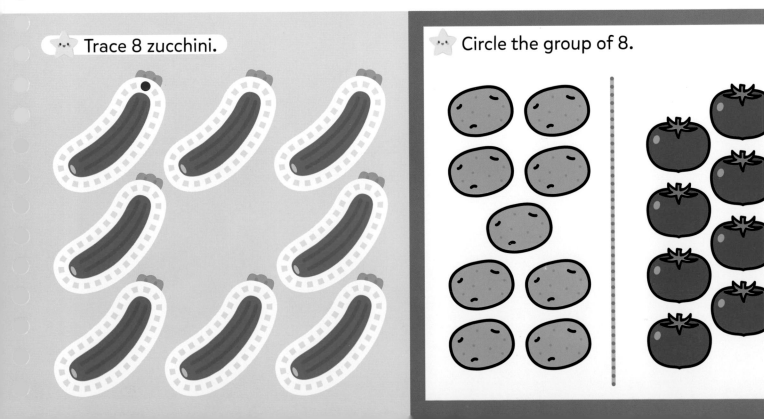

71

Color the circles and count them.

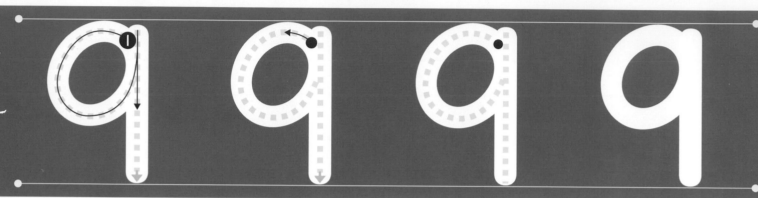

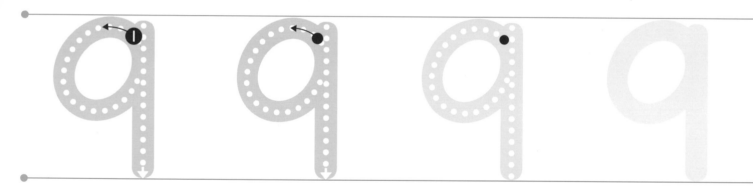

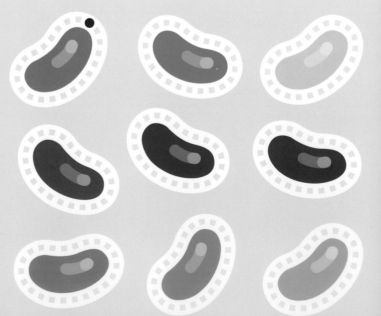

Trace 9 jelly beans.

Circle the group of 9.

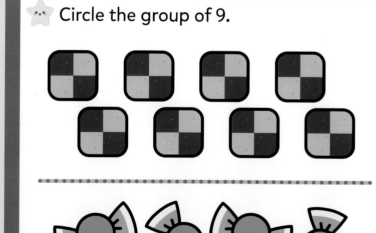

10

ten

Color the circles and count them.

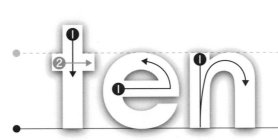

10 10 10 10

10 10 10 10

Trace 10 ladybugs.

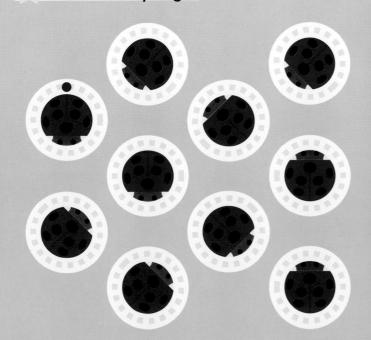

Circle the group of 10.

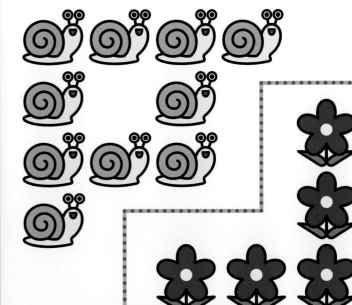

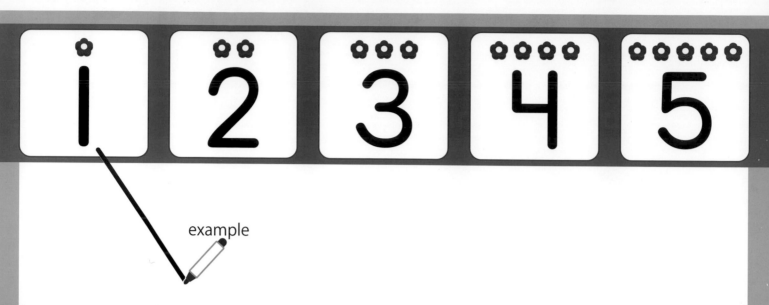

example

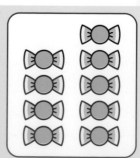

Say the numbers in order from 1 to 10. Then, trace the numbers below.

1→2→3→4→5→6→7→8→9→10

1 2 3 4

5 6 7

8 9 10

Draw lines from 1 to 5 in order.

 1 → 2 → 3 → 4 → 5

Draw lines from 1 to 10 in order.

 1 3 5 7 9

2 4 6 8 10

circle

square

triangle

rectangle

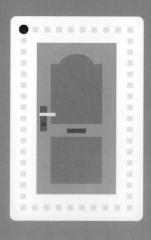
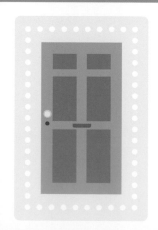
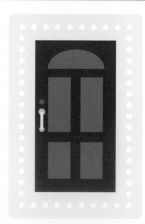

semicircle

diamond

heart

star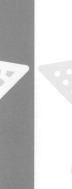

Practice writing your name and age.

First, write your child's name. Then, have your child try to write it.

My name is...

I am...

2 3 4

years old.

78

Remove this page from the book and tack it on the wall.

apple — Aa

bear — Bb

cat — Cc

dog — Dd

elephant — Ee

fish — Ff

giraffe — Gg

hat — Hh

ice cream — Ii

jet — Jj

koala — Kk

lion — Ll

monkey — Mm

necklace — Nn

octopus — Oo

penguin — Pp

queen — Qq

rabbit — Rr

strawberry — Ss

tree — Tt

umbrella — Uu

violin — Vv

whale — Ww

X-ray — Xx

yo-yo — Yy

zebra — Zz

ZOO

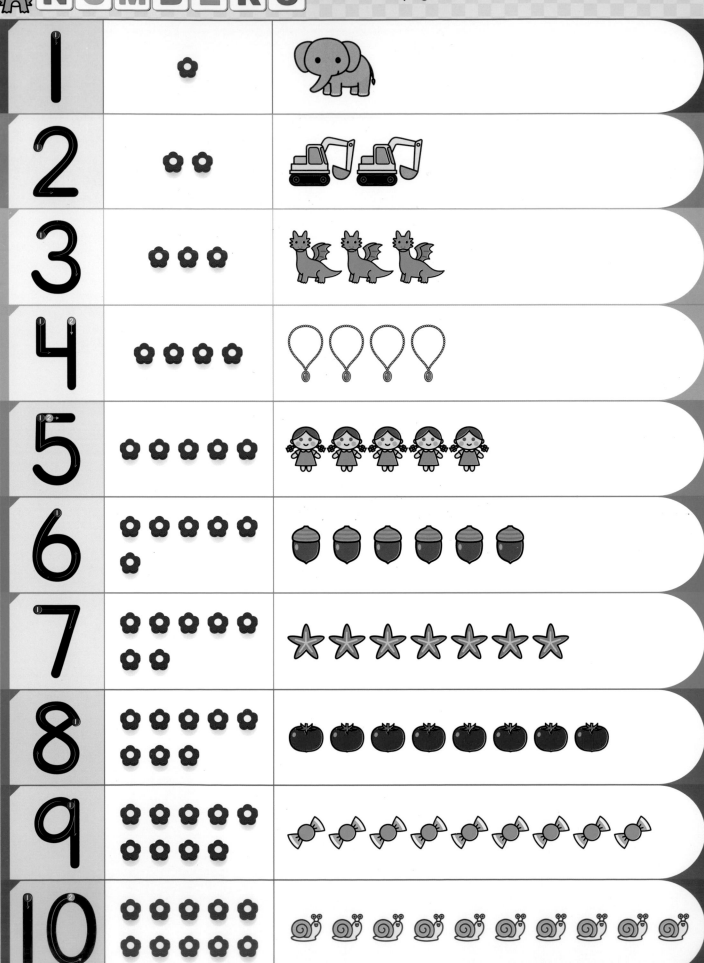